AI Disclaimer

The content provided in "Mastering the Market: Strategies for Success in Stock, Tech, and Real Estate Investing" is for informational and educational purposes only. While we strive to present accurate and up-to-date information, investing in stocks, technology, and real estate involves substantial risk and can result in significant financial loss. The strategies and insights shared within this material reflect the opinions and experiences of the authors and contributors and should not be construed as financial advice. Individual investment decisions should be based on thorough research and, if necessary, consultation with a qualified financial advisor. Past performance is not indicative of future results. There are no guarantees of success, and individuals may experience different outcomes based on a variety of factors, including market conditions, economic changes, and personal financial circumstances. By participating in this program or utilizing its materials, you acknowledge that you are fully responsible for your investment decisions and any associated risks. The authors, publishers, and affiliated parties are not liable for any losses or damages resulting from your reliance on the information provided. Invest wisely and conduct your own due diligence.

Table Of Contents

Chapter 2: The Best Strategy to Be a Great Stock, Tech, and Real Estate Investor 2

Chapter 3: Sustainable Investing Strategies in Tech and Real Estate 2

Chapter 4: Behavioral Finance: Psychology of Successful Investors 2

Chapter 5: Impact of Economic Indicators on Stock Market Decisions 2

Chapter 6: Leveraging Technology for Real-Time Market Analysis . 2

Chapter 7: Diversification Techniques Across Asset Classes 2

Chapter 8: Risk Management Methods for Tech and Real Estate Investments 2

Chapter 9: Long-Term vs. Short-Term Investment Strategies 2

Chapter 10: The Role of Data Analytics in Investment Decisions 2

Chapter 11: Strategies for Identifying Emerging Markets in Tech 2

Chapter 12: Ethical Considerations in Real Estate Investment Practices 2

Chapter 13: Conclusion: The Path to Investment Mastery 2

Chapter 1: Introduction to Market Mastery 1

Chapter 1: Introduction to Market Mastery

Understanding the Investment Landscape

Understanding the investment landscape is essential for any investor seeking success in stock, tech, and real estate markets. The interplay between these sectors creates a dynamic environment influenced by economic indicators, technological advancements, and shifting market sentiments. Investors must familiarize themselves with these elements to navigate the complexities of the investment landscape effectively. An understanding of how various asset classes interact allows for informed decision-making, aligning strategies with market trends and individual investment goals.

Sustainable investing has emerged as a significant trend in both the tech and real estate sectors. Investors are increasingly drawn to opportunities that not only promise financial returns but also contribute positively to society and the environment. In real estate, this could mean investing in energy-efficient properties or developments that prioritize sustainability. In tech, it involves supporting companies that focus on green technologies or ethical data practices. By embracing sustainable investing strategies, investors can position themselves at the forefront of a growing market while aligning their portfolios with ethical considerations.

Behavioral finance plays a crucial role in understanding the psychology behind investment decisions. Successful investors recognize the impact of emotions and cognitive biases on their choices. They strive to maintain a disciplined approach, avoiding impulsive decisions driven by fear or greed. By cultivating a mindset that values patience and long-term vision, investors can enhance their performance in volatile markets. Recognizing common psychological pitfalls allows for better risk management and can lead to more rational, calculated investment strategies.

Economic indicators significantly influence stock market decisions and overall investment strategies. Metrics such as interest rates, inflation rates, and employment statistics provide valuable insights into market conditions. Investors who stay informed about these indicators can better anticipate market movements and adjust their strategies accordingly. For instance, a rise in interest rates might signal a shift in investment focus from high-growth tech stocks to more stable dividend-paying equities. Understanding these indicators allows investors to make proactive decisions rather than reactive ones.

Leveraging technology is vital for real-time market analysis and staying ahead in today's fast-paced investment environment. Tools such as data analytics, algorithmic trading, and market sentiment analysis provide investors with actionable insights and help identify emerging trends. By utilizing these technologies, investors can enhance their ability to make informed decisions quickly, whether they are day trading or managing a long-term portfolio. Moreover, integrating technological tools with traditional investment strategies can foster diversification across asset classes, ultimately leading to improved risk management and investment outcomes.

Importance of Strategy in Investing

Strategy plays a crucial role in investing, serving as the backbone for decision-making across various asset classes, including real estate, stocks, and technology. A well-defined strategy allows investors to navigate the complexities of the market with confidence and clarity. In the fast-paced environments typical of day trading and tech investments, a solid strategy can differentiate between success and failure. Investors who adopt a strategic approach are better equipped to withstand market volatility and capitalize on emerging opportunities, ensuring that their investment decisions align with their long-term financial goals.

In the realm of sustainable investing, strategy is essential for identifying opportunities that not only yield financial returns but also create positive societal impacts. For example, real estate investors can focus on properties that meet green building standards, attracting environmentally conscious tenants and buyers. Similarly, tech investors can prioritize companies that are innovating in ways that promote sustainability. By incorporating ethical considerations into their strategies, investors can align their portfolios with their values while still achieving competitive returns, demonstrating that profitability and responsibility can coexist.

The psychological aspects of investing also underscore the importance of strategy. Behavioral finance highlights how emotions and cognitive biases can cloud investment decisions, leading to impulsive actions that undermine long-term success. A disciplined strategy helps investors remain focused on their objectives, mitigating the influence of short-term market fluctuations and personal biases. By adhering to a systematic investment approach, individuals can better manage their emotional responses, enhancing their ability to make rational decisions based on data and analysis rather than fear or greed.

Economic indicators significantly impact investment strategies, particularly in stock and real estate markets. Investors must remain attuned to these indicators, such as interest rates, unemployment rates, and GDP growth, as they can signal shifts in market conditions. A robust investment strategy incorporates these factors, allowing investors to adjust their portfolios proactively rather than reactively. By understanding how economic variables interact with market dynamics, investors can position themselves advantageously, whether through diversification across asset classes or through tactical asset allocation.

Finally, leveraging technology for real-time market analysis is a critical component of an effective investment strategy. In today's data-driven environment, tools such as advanced analytics, algorithmic trading, and market sentiment analysis provide investors with insights that can significantly enhance decision-making. Investors who harness these technologies can identify trends and emerging markets in tech and real estate more effectively, ultimately gaining a competitive edge. By integrating technology into their strategies, investors can respond to market changes with agility, ensuring that they remain relevant and successful in an ever-evolving investment landscape.

Chapter 2: The Best Strategy to Be a Great Stock, Tech, and Real Estate Investor

Core Principles of Effective Investing

Core principles of effective investing serve as the foundation for successful financial strategies across various sectors, including real estate, stocks, and technology. One of the primary tenets of effective investing is the importance of thorough research and analysis. Investors must be diligent in their examination of market trends, economic indicators, and the specific characteristics of the assets they are considering. This involves not only understanding the financial metrics but also the broader economic environment that influences market behaviors. By leveraging data analytics and technology, investors can gain insights that help them make informed decisions, identify emerging markets, and anticipate shifts in market dynamics.

Another crucial principle is diversification, which plays a significant role in mitigating risk. By spreading investments across various asset classes—stocks, real estate, and tech—investors can protect themselves from the volatility of any single market. Diversification helps to balance potential losses in one area with gains in another. Moreover, within each asset class, investors should consider diversifying their portfolios among different sectors and geographic regions. This strategy not only enhances the potential for returns but also aligns with sustainable investing practices that prioritize environmental, social, and governance (ESG) factors.

Risk management is equally vital in effective investing. Investors must develop robust risk assessment frameworks that account for their financial goals, risk tolerance, and market conditions. This includes implementing strategies such as stop-loss orders in day trading or setting financial thresholds in real estate investments. By adopting a proactive approach to risk, investors can protect their capital and ensure long-term viability. Moreover, understanding behavioral finance can aid investors in recognizing their psychological biases, enabling them to make more rational choices and avoid emotional decision-making during market fluctuations.

Long-term versus short-term investment strategies is another area where effective principles come into play. While day trading may focus on quick gains from market movements, long-term investing emphasizes the importance of patience and a broader view of market cycles. Investors who adopt a long-term perspective often benefit from compounding returns and are less affected by short-term volatility. It is essential for investors to align their strategies with their personal financial objectives and to remain disciplined in executing their plans, regardless of market noise.

Finally, ethical considerations should be at the forefront of all investment decisions. Investors in real estate and technology sectors must be aware of the societal impacts of their investments. This includes considering the implications of gentrification in real estate projects and the ethical use of technology in business practices. By adhering to ethical standards, investors not only contribute positively to society but also enhance their reputation and foster trust with stakeholders. Integrating these core principles into investment practices can lead to sustainable success in the ever-evolving landscape of finance and investment.

Building a Holistic Investment Portfolio

Building a holistic investment portfolio requires a strategic approach that encompasses various asset classes, including stocks, technology, and real estate. Investors must first assess their individual risk tolerance, investment horizon, and financial goals. By understanding these personal factors, investors can begin to allocate their resources in a manner that aligns with their objectives. A well-structured portfolio not only balances risk and return but also positions investors to take advantage of market fluctuations across different sectors.

Diversification is a fundamental principle in constructing a resilient investment portfolio. Investors should consider spreading their investments across various asset classes to mitigate risks associated with market volatility. For instance, combining equities with real estate holdings can provide a buffer during economic downturns, as these assets often respond differently to market conditions. Additionally, incorporating tech investments can enhance growth potential, particularly in a rapidly evolving digital landscape. By diversifying investments, investors can safeguard their portfolios against unforeseen market shifts while capturing opportunities across sectors.

In the realm of sustainable investing, it is essential to integrate environmental, social, and governance (ESG) criteria into the portfolio-building process. Investors increasingly seek to align their financial goals with their ethical values, particularly in tech and real estate sectors. By investing in companies that prioritize sustainability, investors not only contribute to positive societal impact but also tap into a growing market trend. This approach can lead to long-term financial performance, as businesses that adopt sustainable practices often experience increased consumer loyalty and reduced operational risks.

Behavioral finance plays a significant role in shaping investment decisions. Understanding the psychological biases that can affect investor behavior is crucial for maintaining a disciplined investment strategy. For example, the tendency to overreact to market news can lead to poor decision-making, such as panic selling or impulsive buying. By cultivating awareness of these biases and employing strategies that promote rational decision-making, investors can enhance their ability to navigate the complexities of the market. This psychological resilience is particularly vital in volatile environments, where emotional reactions can undermine sound investment principles.

Finally, leveraging technology for real-time market analysis can greatly enhance investment decision-making. Advanced data analytics tools provide investors with insights into market trends, economic indicators, and emerging opportunities in tech and real estate. By utilizing these resources, investors can make informed decisions, identify potential risks, and pinpoint emerging markets that present growth potential. The integration of technology into the investment process not only streamlines analysis but also empowers investors to respond proactively to changing market dynamics, ensuring that their portfolios remain aligned with their strategic objectives.

Chapter 3: Sustainable Investing Strategies in Tech and Real Estate

Defining Sustainable Investing

Sustainable investing is an investment strategy that integrates environmental, social, and governance (ESG) factors into the decision-making process. This approach seeks not only financial returns but also positive societal impact, appealing to a growing demographic of investors who are conscious of the implications of their capital allocation. For real estate investors and those in the tech sector, understanding sustainable investing can enhance portfolio performance while contributing to a more sustainable economy.

The increasing awareness of climate change, social justice, and corporate governance has propelled sustainable investing into the mainstream, making it a crucial consideration for modern investors.

In the realm of real estate, sustainable investing encompasses various practices, such as the development of energy-efficient buildings, the use of sustainable materials, and the promotion of social equity in housing. Investors are recognizing that properties designed with sustainability in mind often yield higher returns over time, as they attract environmentally conscious tenants and buyers. Additionally, sustainable real estate projects can reduce operational costs through energy savings and can benefit from government incentives aimed at promoting green development. This alignment of financial prudence and ethical responsibility positions sustainable real estate investments favorably in a competitive market.

For tech investors, sustainable investing can manifest in the funding of companies that prioritize environmental stewardship and social responsibility. The tech industry has a unique opportunity to drive innovation in sustainability through the development of green technology and clean energy solutions. Investors can leverage data analytics to identify emerging markets and technologies that focus on sustainability, thus aligning their portfolios with future growth areas. As consumers increasingly demand sustainable products and services, tech companies that adopt sustainable practices are more likely to succeed, presenting a compelling case for investors.

Behavioral finance plays a significant role in sustainable investing, as investors' decisions are often influenced by personal values and social considerations. Understanding the psychology behind investment choices can help investors navigate the complexities of sustainable investing. Many investors find that aligning their portfolios with their values not only fulfills a moral obligation but also enhances their overall satisfaction and commitment to their investment strategies. This connection between values and investment decisions can lead to a more resilient investment approach, particularly in times of market volatility.

As sustainable investing continues to evolve, it is essential for investors to adopt risk management methods that account for the unique challenges associated with this approach. Diversification across asset classes, including sustainable real estate and tech investments, can mitigate risks while capitalizing on the growth potential of sustainable markets. Moreover, leveraging technology for real-time market analysis can provide insights into the performance of sustainable investments, helping investors make informed decisions in a rapidly changing landscape. The intersection of sustainability, technology, and strategic investing presents a compelling opportunity for those looking to master the market while making a positive impact.

Integration of ESG Criteria in Investment Decisions

The integration of Environmental, Social, and Governance (ESG) criteria in investment decisions has emerged as a critical focus for investors across various asset classes, including real estate, stocks, and technology. As awareness of global sustainability challenges grows, investors are increasingly recognizing that financial performance is intertwined with social responsibility and environmental stewardship. This shift is not merely a trend but a strategic approach that aligns with the evolving values of consumers and investors alike. For real estate investors, incorporating ESG principles can enhance property value, attract tenants, and reduce operational risks, while stock and tech investors can mitigate reputational risks and capitalize on innovative solutions addressing social and environmental issues.

Real estate investors can leverage ESG criteria by assessing properties based on their energy efficiency, sustainability practices, and community impact. Buildings that adhere to green standards not only reduce operating costs through lower energy consumption but also appeal to a market increasingly driven by eco-conscious consumers and businesses. The demand for sustainable properties is steadily rising, as companies seek to enhance their corporate social responsibility profiles. By focusing on ESG factors, real estate investors can differentiate their portfolios, increase occupancy rates, and potentially achieve higher returns in the long run.

For stock and tech investors, the integration of ESG criteria involves analyzing companies based on their environmental impact, social policies, and governance practices. Firms that prioritize sustainability are often better positioned to manage risks associated with regulatory changes, resource scarcity, and shifting consumer preferences. Moreover, companies with strong governance practices tend to exhibit better management and operational efficiencies, leading to improved financial performance. Investors who actively seek out ESG-compliant companies may find opportunities in emerging markets where sustainable technology and practices are gaining traction, presenting prospects for significant growth.

Day traders and stock brokers also stand to benefit from the incorporation of ESG metrics into their trading strategies. By utilizing real-time data analytics, traders can identify market trends that reflect broader societal shifts towards sustainability. Understanding how ESG factors influence stock prices can provide valuable insights, enabling traders to make informed decisions that align with both ethical considerations and profit potential. Furthermore, the growing demand for ESG-focused investment products, including exchange-traded funds and mutual funds, offers traders a pathway to diversify their portfolios while adhering to sustainable investing principles.

Ultimately, the successful integration of ESG criteria into investment decisions requires a systematic approach that combines risk management, behavioral finance insights, and a forward-looking perspective on economic indicators. By embracing this holistic investment strategy, investors in real estate, stocks, and technology can not only contribute positively to society and the environment but also position themselves strategically in a rapidly changing market landscape. The transition towards sustainable investing is not merely an ethical choice; it is a comprehensive strategy that aligns with the long-term interests of investors and the communities they serve.

Chapter 4: Behavioral Finance: Psychology of Successful Investors

Common Cognitive Biases in Investing

Cognitive biases can significantly impact decision-making processes in investing, often leading to irrational choices that undermine financial success. One of the most prevalent biases is confirmation bias, where investors favor information that confirms their existing beliefs while disregarding contradictory evidence. This can be particularly detrimental in fast-paced environments like day trading or tech investing, where the ability to adapt to new information is crucial. For instance, a stock trader may focus exclusively on positive trends of a particular technology stock, ignoring negative news that could signal a downturn. This selective perception can lead to poor investment decisions, as it prevents a comprehensive evaluation of all relevant data.

Another common bias is overconfidence, which often manifests when investors overestimate their knowledge or ability to predict market movements. This is especially apparent in the realm of real estate investing, where successful past experiences may lead investors to take excessive risks. Overconfidence can result in underestimating market volatility or ignoring essential due diligence, leading to significant financial losses. A prudent approach requires acknowledging the inherent uncertainty in markets and avoiding the temptation to act on gut feelings rather than thorough analysis.

Anchoring is another cognitive bias that can hinder effective investment strategies. This occurs when investors fixate on a specific reference point, such as the initial purchase price of a stock or property, and allow that anchor to distort their perception of its current value. For example, a stock investor might hold onto a declining asset because they are anchored to its previous high price, failing to recognize the changing market conditions. This bias can prevent timely selling decisions and inhibit the ability to capitalize on more promising opportunities.

Loss aversion, the tendency to prefer avoiding losses over acquiring equivalent gains, significantly affects investment behavior. Investors often react more strongly to potential losses than to potential gains, leading to overly cautious strategies. In the context of real estate or stock investments, this can manifest as holding onto underperforming assets in hopes of breaking even, rather than reallocating resources to more fruitful ventures. Understanding the psychological impact of loss aversion can help investors take a more balanced approach, focusing on long-term growth instead of short-term setbacks.

Finally, the herd mentality can lead to irrational market behaviors, particularly in volatile segments like technology stocks or emerging markets. When investors follow the crowd, they often make decisions based on social influences rather than fundamental analysis. This can result in inflated asset prices during market booms and panic selling during downturns. To counteract herd behavior, investors should cultivate independent research habits and rely on data-driven strategies, ensuring that decisions are grounded in sound analysis rather than collective emotional responses. Recognizing and mitigating these common cognitive biases can enhance investment outcomes across various asset classes, promoting a more rational and sustainable approach to investing.

Developing a Growth Mindset for Investment Success

Developing a growth mindset is essential for achieving success in the dynamic fields of real estate and stock investing. A growth mindset, characterized by the belief that abilities and intelligence can be developed through dedication and hard work, fosters resilience and adaptability. In the context of investing, this perspective encourages investors to view challenges and setbacks as opportunities for learning rather than insurmountable obstacles. By embracing this mindset, investors can enhance their decision-making processes, leading to more informed and strategic actions in the unpredictable markets of real estate and technology.

One key aspect of cultivating a growth mindset is the importance of continuous learning. The investment landscape is constantly evolving, influenced by technological advancements, economic indicators, and shifts in consumer behavior. Successful investors prioritize staying informed about market trends and emerging sectors. They engage in activities such as attending workshops, reading industry publications, and participating in online forums. This commitment to education not only expands their knowledge base but also helps them remain agile and ready to pivot their strategies as new information becomes available.

Behavioral finance plays a significant role in shaping an investor's mindset. Understanding the psychological biases that can cloud judgment is crucial for maintaining a growth-oriented approach. Investors often face emotional responses to market fluctuations, which can lead to impulsive decisions. By recognizing these biases, such as overconfidence or loss aversion, investors can develop strategies to mitigate their effects. This self-awareness enables them to remain focused on long-term goals and make decisions based on data and analysis rather than emotional reactions, ultimately contributing to a more disciplined investment strategy.

Another vital component of a growth mindset is the willingness to embrace risk and learn from failures. In both real estate and stock investing, risk is an inherent part of the process. Investors who adopt a growth mindset view losses not as failures but as valuable lessons. By analyzing what went wrong and applying those insights to future investments, they can refine their strategies and improve their chances of success. This iterative approach fosters resilience, enabling investors to navigate market fluctuations with a sense of confidence and purpose.

Finally, leveraging technology plays a pivotal role in developing a growth mindset for investment success. The integration of data analytics and real-time market analysis provides investors with the tools needed to make informed decisions. By utilizing advanced technologies, such as machine learning algorithms and predictive analytics, investors can identify emerging markets and trends, enhancing their ability to diversify across asset classes. This technological edge not only streamlines the investment process but also cultivates a mindset that embraces innovation and adaptability, essential traits for thriving in today's competitive investment landscape.

Chapter 5: Impact of Economic Indicators on Stock Market Decisions

Key Economic Indicators to Monitor

Key economic indicators serve as vital signposts for investors navigating the complex landscapes of stock, tech, and real estate markets. Understanding these indicators can provide insights into market trends and potential investment opportunities. Among the most critical indicators are GDP growth rates, unemployment rates, inflation rates, interest rates, and consumer confidence indices. Each of these elements not only reflects the current economic environment but also influences investor behavior and market dynamics.

Gross Domestic Product (GDP) growth rates are foundational for understanding the overall health of the economy. A rising GDP typically signals a robust economy, which can lead to increased corporate earnings and, consequently, higher stock prices. For real estate investors, GDP growth can indicate a stronger demand for housing and commercial properties, as more people are employed and have disposable income. Conversely, a declining GDP can signal economic downturns, prompting investors to evaluate their portfolios and consider protective strategies.

The unemployment rate is another crucial indicator that impacts consumer spending and investment decisions. High unemployment often reduces disposable income, leading to lower demand for goods and services, including real estate. Investors should monitor employment trends, as a decrease in unemployment may correlate with increased consumer confidence and spending, creating favorable conditions for both stock and real estate investments. Understanding the cyclical nature of employment can help investors anticipate market shifts and position themselves accordingly.

Inflation rates and interest rates are intertwined and play a significant role in investment strategies. Rising inflation can erode purchasing power and prompt central banks to increase interest rates, which can adversely affect borrowing costs for real estate and tech investments. Investors should be vigilant about inflation trends, as they can lead to volatility in both stock and real estate markets. By tracking these rates, investors can adjust their portfolios to mitigate risks associated with rising costs and interest expenses.

Finally, the consumer confidence index provides valuable insights into the sentiments of the general populace regarding economic conditions. High consumer confidence often leads to increased spending, benefiting sectors like retail and real estate. Conversely, low confidence can signal potential downturns, prompting investors to reassess their strategies. Keeping an eye on consumer sentiment can enhance decision-making processes, especially when combined with data analytics and technology tools that facilitate real-time market analysis.

In conclusion, monitoring these key economic indicators is essential for investors aiming to make informed decisions in the stock, tech, and real estate markets. By understanding the implications of GDP growth, unemployment rates, inflation, interest rates, and consumer confidence, investors can develop sustainable strategies that align with market conditions. This informed approach not only enhances investment outcomes but also fosters resilience against economic fluctuations, ultimately leading to long-term success.

Interpreting Economic Data for Investment Strategy

Interpreting economic data is a critical skill for investors in real estate, stocks, and technology sectors. Economic indicators such as GDP growth, employment rates, inflation, and interest rates provide essential insights into market conditions. For real estate investors, understanding regional economic trends can reveal potential property appreciation or depreciation. Similarly, stock investors can gauge the overall health of the market and adjust their strategies accordingly. By analyzing these indicators, investors can make informed decisions that align with their investment goals and risk tolerance.

An important aspect of interpreting economic data is recognizing the relationship between various indicators. For example, rising interest rates can indicate a tightening monetary policy aimed at controlling inflation, which may lead to reduced consumer spending. This can negatively impact both the real estate market and stock prices. On the other hand, a strong jobs report may suggest increasing consumer confidence, leading to higher demand in both real estate and the tech sector. By understanding these connections, investors can anticipate market trends and position their portfolios to capitalize on emerging opportunities.

Behavioral finance plays a significant role in how investors interpret and react to economic data. Cognitive biases, such as overreacting to short-term data or confirmation bias, can cloud judgment and lead to poor investment decisions. Successful investors recognize these psychological factors and strive to base their strategies on a disciplined analysis of economic indicators, rather than emotional reactions. By maintaining a focus on long-term trends and avoiding knee-jerk responses to market fluctuations, investors can enhance their decision-making processes.

The advent of technology has revolutionized the way investors analyze economic data. Real-time market analysis tools and data analytics platforms empower investors to access vast amounts of information quickly, allowing for more timely and informed decisions. Investors in the tech sector, in particular, can leverage these tools to identify trends and emerging markets, ensuring they remain competitive. Furthermore, by utilizing data analytics, investors can develop sophisticated models to predict market movements and assess the potential impact of economic indicators on their investment strategies.

Ultimately, an effective investment strategy requires a comprehensive understanding of economic data and its implications. Whether investing in stocks, technology, or real estate, investors must remain vigilant and adaptable, continuously analyzing how economic indicators affect their chosen markets. By developing a systematic approach to interpreting economic data and integrating it into their overall investment strategy, investors can enhance their chances of long-term success while navigating the complexities of the financial landscape.

Chapter 6: Leveraging Technology for Real-Time Market Analysis

Tools for Real-Time Market Tracking

In the fast-paced environment of investing, having the right tools for real-time market tracking is essential for success. Investors in real estate, stocks, and technology must be equipped with platforms that provide up-to-the-minute data and analytics. These tools facilitate timely decision-making, allowing investors to respond quickly to market changes. Features like live price feeds, customizable dashboards, and alerts for significant market movements ensure that investors can monitor their investments effectively and capitalize on opportunities as they arise.

One of the most critical aspects of real-time market tracking is the integration of various data sources. Advanced tools aggregate information from multiple platforms, including financial news, social media sentiment, and economic indicators. This holistic view helps investors understand market dynamics better and make informed decisions. By utilizing tools that synthesize diverse data points, investors can gain insights into market trends and potential shifts, which is particularly beneficial for those focusing on sustainable investing strategies in tech and real estate.

Data analytics plays a pivotal role in enhancing investment decisions. Sophisticated software offers analytical capabilities that allow investors to assess historical performance alongside current market conditions. These analytical tools can identify patterns and correlations that might not be immediately apparent. For instance, understanding the impact of economic indicators on stock market movements can guide investors in timing their entries and exits more effectively. Additionally, behavioral finance insights can be integrated into these tools, helping investors recognize psychological biases that may influence their investment choices.

Furthermore, mobile applications have revolutionized real-time market tracking, enabling investors to stay connected regardless of location. With notifications and alerts sent directly to their smartphones, investors can react promptly to critical developments. This immediacy is particularly important for day traders and those involved in high-frequency trading strategies. The convenience of real-time updates allows investors to maintain a competitive edge, making it easier to execute trades based on the latest market information.

Lastly, it is crucial to consider risk management when utilizing real-time market tracking tools. Effective tools not only provide data but also incorporate risk assessment features that help investors evaluate potential losses and gains. By leveraging technology to create diversified portfolios and manage exposure across various asset classes, investors can enhance their overall strategy. This proactive approach to tracking and managing risk ensures that investors are not only reacting to market trends but also strategically positioning themselves for long-term success in their investment endeavors.

Importance of Data Visualization in Decision Making

Data visualization plays a pivotal role in decision-making for investors across stock, tech, and real estate sectors. The ability to transform complex datasets into visual formats facilitates a clearer understanding of market trends, enabling investors to make informed decisions quickly. By employing charts, graphs, and dashboards, investors can easily identify patterns and anomalies that might otherwise be overlooked in raw data. This visual representation not only enhances comprehension but also allows for more efficient communication of findings among stakeholders, ensuring that all parties involved are aligned with the strategic direction.

Investors must navigate vast amounts of data from various sources, including economic indicators, market trends, and company performance metrics. Data visualization tools help distill this information into actionable insights. For instance, heat maps can illustrate property values in real estate, while line graphs can track stock performance over time, helping investors understand volatility and potential future movements. By leveraging these visual tools, investors can focus on critical data points that directly influence their strategies, such as identifying emerging markets in tech or assessing risk in real estate portfolios.

In the realm of behavioral finance, data visualization aids in understanding investor psychology and market sentiment. By visualizing data related to consumer behavior or investor reactions to economic news, investors can better gauge market dynamics and adjust their strategies accordingly. This understanding is crucial when evaluating long-term versus short-term investment strategies, as it provides insight into how market sentiment can impact asset pricing. Effective visualization can reveal trends that align with psychological patterns, equipping investors with the knowledge to make decisions that are both data-driven and emotionally intelligent.

Moreover, with the integration of technology in investment practices, real-time data visualization has become indispensable. Investors can utilize sophisticated platforms that offer live updates on market conditions, enabling them to react swiftly to changes. This real-time analysis is particularly valuable in day trading, where every second counts. By employing visualization techniques that highlight real-time trends, investors can identify opportunities for quick trades or adjust their strategies to mitigate losses, ultimately improving their overall performance in a fast-paced market environment.

Finally, ethical considerations in investment practices underscore the importance of transparency and accountability, which data visualization can support. By clearly presenting data related to investment practices and outcomes, investors can foster trust with stakeholders and clients. This transparency is especially important in sustainable investing strategies, where investors seek to align their financial goals with ethical standards. Visualization tools can help illustrate the impact of investments on social and environmental metrics, enabling investors to make decisions that reflect their values while also achieving financial success. In summary, effective data visualization is essential for informed decision-making across the investment landscape, enabling investors to navigate complexities with clarity and confidence.

Chapter 7: Diversification Techniques Across Asset Classes

Benefits of Diversification

Diversification is a fundamental principle in investment strategy that significantly impacts risk management and overall portfolio performance. For real estate investors, day traders, stock investors, stock brokers, and professionals in the tech industry, understanding the benefits of diversification can lead to more informed decisions and enhanced financial stability. By distributing investments across various asset classes, sectors, and geographic regions, investors can mitigate the effects of volatility and reduce the risk associated with concentrated holdings. This approach ensures that a downturn in one area does not disproportionately affect the entire portfolio, ultimately leading to more sustainable investment outcomes.

One of the primary advantages of diversification is its ability to lower the overall risk profile of an investment portfolio. In real estate, for instance, investing in multiple properties across different markets can shield an investor from local economic downturns. Similarly, stock investors can reduce the impact of poor performance from a single stock by spreading their investments across different sectors and industries. This risk management technique is particularly crucial in today's rapidly changing economic landscape, where market conditions can shift unexpectedly. By diversifying their investments, traders and investors can better navigate uncertainty and protect their capital.

Moreover, diversification can enhance the potential for returns by capitalizing on various growth opportunities. Different asset classes often perform differently under varying economic conditions. For example, while tech stocks may thrive in a booming economy, real estate investments may offer stability during economic downturns. By strategically diversifying their portfolios, investors can position themselves to benefit from the strengths of multiple asset classes. This balanced approach allows them to capture gains from different sectors, ultimately leading to more consistent long-term performance.

In the context of behavioral finance, diversification also plays a crucial role in mitigating emotional decision-making. Investors who hold concentrated positions may react more strongly to market fluctuations, leading to impulsive decisions driven by fear or greed. By diversifying their portfolios, investors can foster a sense of security and confidence, enabling them to make more rational decisions based on data and analysis rather than emotional responses. This psychological advantage can be significant in volatile markets, where maintaining a level-headed approach is essential for success.

Finally, leveraging technology for real-time market analysis can further enhance the benefits of diversification. Advanced data analytics tools allow investors to monitor various asset classes and market trends simultaneously, identifying emerging opportunities and potential risks. By integrating technology into their investment strategies, real estate investors, stock traders, and brokers can make more informed decisions about how to diversify their portfolios effectively. This capability not only improves risk management but also empowers investors to adapt their strategies based on real-time data, maximizing their chances for success in an ever-evolving market landscape.

Strategies for Effective Asset Allocation

Effective asset allocation is a cornerstone of successful investing, particularly in complex fields such as real estate, stocks, and technology. Investors must craft a strategy that balances risk and return while aligning with their financial goals and market conditions. A thorough understanding of various asset classes and their interrelationships is essential. By employing a diversified portfolio, investors can mitigate risks associated with market volatility and economic fluctuations. This approach not only enhances potential returns but also allows for greater resilience in the face of unexpected market shifts.

One of the key strategies for effective asset allocation is diversification across different asset classes. This involves spreading investments across stocks, bonds, real estate, and alternative assets to reduce the impact of poor performance in any single category. For real estate investors, this might mean investing in residential properties, commercial real estate, and real estate investment trusts (REITs). Stock investors, on the other hand, can diversify within sectors, such as technology, healthcare, and consumer goods, to capitalize on sector-specific trends while minimizing exposure to sector downturns. By carefully selecting a mix of assets, investors can achieve a more stable overall portfolio performance.

Risk management plays a critical role in the asset allocation process. Investors must assess their risk tolerance and adjust their portfolios accordingly. Techniques such as stop-loss orders, options trading, and the use of market hedges can help protect investments from sudden downturns. For tech and real estate sectors, where market dynamics can change rapidly due to technological advancements or regulatory shifts, having a robust risk management framework is vital. Regularly reviewing and rebalancing the portfolio ensures that the asset allocation remains aligned with the investor's risk profile and market conditions.

Leveraging technology for real-time market analysis is another effective strategy for asset allocation. Investors can utilize data analytics tools and platforms that provide insights into market trends, economic indicators, and emerging opportunities. For instance, applying machine learning algorithms can help identify patterns in stock price movements or real estate valuations. By staying informed and agile, investors can make timely adjustments to their asset allocations, capitalizing on short-term opportunities while maintaining a long-term investment strategy.

Lastly, understanding the psychological aspects of investing, as highlighted by behavioral finance, is crucial for effective asset allocation. Investors often face emotional biases that can cloud their judgment, leading to suboptimal decisions. By recognizing these biases and adopting a disciplined investment approach, investors can make more rational choices regarding asset allocation. Strategies such as setting predefined investment criteria, utilizing automated trading systems, and maintaining a long-term perspective can help mitigate the impact of emotional decision-making, ultimately leading to more successful investment outcomes in the stock, tech, and real estate markets.

Chapter 8: Risk Management Methods for Tech and Real Estate Investments

Identifying and Assessing Investment Risks

Identifying and assessing investment risks is a critical component for anyone involved in real estate, day trading, or stock investing. Each asset class presents unique challenges and uncertainties that can significantly impact returns. Real estate investors must navigate market fluctuations, property valuation changes, and regulatory shifts, while stock traders face volatility influenced by economic indicators and market sentiment. Understanding these risks involves analyzing external factors and internal decision-making processes that can lead to more informed and effective investment strategies.

A fundamental step in risk assessment is determining the potential impact of economic indicators on investment performance. For stock and tech investors, this includes monitoring interest rates, inflation rates, and employment data, which can drive market trends and investor sentiment. Real estate investors must also consider these indicators, as they can affect property demand and rental income. By staying informed about macroeconomic conditions, investors can better anticipate market movements and adjust their strategies accordingly.

Behavioral finance plays a significant role in risk identification, as psychological factors often drive investment decisions. Investors can fall prey to cognitive biases such as overconfidence or herd mentality, which may cloud their judgment and lead to suboptimal investment choices. By being aware of these biases, investors can implement techniques to mitigate their influence, such as establishing clear investment criteria and relying on data analytics. This approach enhances decision-making and helps maintain a disciplined investment strategy, ultimately reducing exposure to unnecessary risks.

Diversification techniques across asset classes are essential for managing risk effectively. Investors should consider spreading their portfolios across stocks, real estate, and tech investments, as each area reacts differently to market conditions. This strategy not only helps in risk reduction but also enhances the potential for returns, especially in volatile markets. By strategically allocating resources, investors can cushion their portfolios against downturns in any single market while capitalizing on emerging opportunities across sectors.

Finally, leveraging technology for real-time market analysis can significantly enhance risk assessment capabilities. Advanced tools and platforms provide investors with immediate access to market data, trends, and analytics, enabling them to make informed decisions quickly. This real-time insight is invaluable in fast-moving environments, such as day trading or tech investments, where timing can be crucial. By integrating technology into their investment processes, investors can better identify potential risks, monitor their portfolios continuously, and adjust their strategies to align with changing market conditions.

Strategies for Mitigating Risks

Strategies for mitigating risks in investing encompass a range of techniques tailored to address the inherent uncertainties of stock, tech, and real estate markets. One fundamental approach is diversification, which involves spreading investments across various asset classes and sectors. By diversifying, investors can reduce the impact of poor performance in any one area on their overall portfolio. This strategy not only mitigates risk but also enhances the potential for returns, as different asset classes often respond differently to economic changes and market fluctuations.

Another critical risk management method is the implementation of stop-loss orders in stock trading. These orders allow investors to set predetermined exit points for their investments, effectively capping potential losses. This strategy is particularly useful in the volatile nature of day trading and stock investments, where market conditions can change rapidly. Additionally, real estate investors can use similar principles by performing comprehensive market analysis and setting financial thresholds that trigger a reevaluation of property investments, helping to avoid significant losses.

Behavioral finance plays a significant role in understanding and mitigating risks. Investors often fall prey to psychological biases that can cloud their judgment, leading to impulsive decisions. Educating oneself about common biases, such as herd mentality or loss aversion, can enhance decision-making processes. By fostering a disciplined investment approach and adhering to a well-defined strategy, investors can better navigate emotional responses and maintain focus on long-term goals rather than short-term market movements.

Leveraging technology is another effective strategy for risk mitigation. Advanced data analytics tools enable investors to analyze market trends in real-time, providing insights that can inform more strategic decisions. For tech investors, utilizing algorithms and artificial intelligence to forecast market shifts can be particularly beneficial. In the realm of real estate, technology can assist in analyzing property values, rental income potential, and neighborhood trends, equipping investors with the necessary information to minimize risks associated with property investments.

Lastly, staying informed about economic indicators is vital for making sound investment decisions. Understanding how factors such as interest rates, inflation, and employment rates impact market dynamics can guide investors in adjusting their strategies proactively. This knowledge allows for timely actions, such as reallocating assets or pivoting investment focuses in response to changing economic conditions. By integrating these strategies, real estate investors, stock traders, and tech investors can develop a robust framework for mitigating risks and enhancing their investment outcomes.

Chapter 9: Long-Term vs. Short-Term Investment Strategies

Pros and Cons of Long-Term Investing

Long-term investing is a strategy that can yield significant benefits for investors in various sectors like real estate, stocks, and technology. One of the primary advantages of this approach is the potential for compound growth. By holding investments over an extended period, investors can benefit from the appreciation of asset values and reinvestment of dividends or income. This strategy allows for the maximization of returns, as the compounding effect can substantially increase wealth over time. Additionally, long-term investing often reduces the impact of market volatility, enabling investors to ride out short-term fluctuations without succumbing to panic selling.

However, long-term investing is not without its drawbacks. One of the most significant challenges is the need for patience and discipline. Investors must resist the temptation to react to market downturns or news cycles, which can be psychologically taxing. The emotional aspect of investing can lead to decisions that are not aligned with long-term goals. Furthermore, the opportunity cost associated with locking funds into long-term investments can be substantial, particularly in fast-moving markets like technology, where short-term gains might be more readily available.

Another critical consideration is the potential for changing market conditions to affect long-term investments. Economic indicators, such as interest rates, inflation, and industry trends, can significantly influence asset performance. Real estate, for instance, can be heavily impacted by local economic shifts, while tech investments may be susceptible to rapid advancements in innovation that could render existing products obsolete. Therefore, long-term investors must continuously analyze economic data and market trends to ensure their portfolios remain relevant and competitive.

Despite these challenges, long-term investing can be enhanced through diversification techniques across asset classes. By spreading investments across different sectors—such as combining real estate with stocks and tech—investors can mitigate risks associated with individual market downturns. This strategy not only provides a buffer against volatility but also positions investors to capitalize on emerging markets and sectors as they develop. Effective diversification can lead to a more stable portfolio, which is particularly advantageous for those focused on sustainable investing strategies.

Lastly, leveraging technology for real-time market analysis can greatly benefit long-term investors. Advanced data analytics tools allow investors to monitor trends and economic indicators, providing insights that can inform investment decisions. By integrating technology into their strategies, investors can enhance their understanding of market dynamics and adjust their portfolios accordingly, ensuring they remain aligned with their long-term investment goals. This fusion of traditional investment principles with modern technology creates a robust framework for achieving success in the ever-evolving landscapes of stock, tech, and real estate investing.

Short-Term Trading Techniques and Their Effectiveness

Short-term trading techniques encompass a variety of strategies aimed at capitalizing on market fluctuations within a brief time frame, typically ranging from seconds to a few weeks. For real estate investors, day traders, and stock brokers, these techniques can provide quick returns, but they also introduce a higher level of risk. Techniques such as scalping, momentum trading, and swing trading allow investors to exploit short-lived opportunities driven by market sentiment, news events, or technical indicators. While these strategies can be effective, they require a robust understanding of market dynamics and extensive preparation to identify optimal entry and exit points.

One of the most widely utilized short-term trading techniques is momentum trading, which involves buying securities that are trending upward while selling those that are trending downward. This strategy is particularly appealing to stock investors and day traders because it leverages the collective psychology of the market. When investors recognize a stock's upward trajectory, they often jump on the bandwagon, further driving up prices. However, this technique requires diligent monitoring of market trends and can be impacted by external factors such as economic indicators or earnings announcements, which may alter momentum rapidly.

Scalping is another technique favored by day traders, characterized by making numerous trades throughout the day to capture small price movements. This method demands a high level of precision and speed, as traders aim to profit from minimal price changes. While scalping can be profitable for those with the necessary skills, it also entails significant transaction costs and a need for advanced trading technology to ensure timely execution. Investors must also manage the psychological stress associated with the rapid pace of trading, as even minor mistakes can lead to substantial losses.

Swing trading, on the other hand, allows for a slightly longer investment horizon, typically holding positions for several days to weeks. This technique appeals to both stock investors and real estate investors who may not be able to commit to the constant monitoring required for scalping or momentum trading. Swing trading strategies often rely on technical analysis to identify patterns and potential reversal points. Although this approach can yield significant returns, it still requires traders to stay informed about market trends and developments that may impact their holdings.

Ultimately, the effectiveness of short-term trading techniques hinges on the investor's ability to remain disciplined and informed. While these strategies can offer lucrative opportunities, they also come with increased risks that can affect overall portfolio performance. Investors in real estate and technology sectors must weigh the potential for quick gains against the likelihood of market volatility and consider how these techniques fit into their broader investment strategy. By understanding both the mechanics and psychological aspects of short-term trading, investors can better navigate the complexities of the market and make informed decisions that align with their financial goals.

Chapter 10: The Role of Data Analytics in Investment Decisions

Importance of Data in Modern Investing

In the contemporary landscape of investing, data plays a crucial role in shaping strategies and informing decisions across various sectors, including real estate, stock trading, and technology. The sheer volume of available data allows investors to analyze trends, evaluate potential risks, and identify opportunities with unprecedented precision. Modern investors must harness this wealth of information to enhance their decision-making processes, tailoring their strategies to meet specific goals and navigate the complexities of the market. With the integration of advanced analytics tools, the ability to interpret data effectively can differentiate successful investors from those who struggle to keep pace with the evolving market dynamics.

Investors today rely on data analytics to understand market trends and consumer behavior. By analyzing economic indicators, such as employment rates, inflation, and interest rates, investors can gauge the broader economic environment and its impact on their investments. This insight is particularly vital for real estate investors, who must consider local market conditions, property values, and demographic shifts. Furthermore, stock investors can utilize data to track company performance metrics, enabling them to make informed decisions about buying or selling shares. The ability to correlate various data points helps investors anticipate market movements and adjust their strategies accordingly.

Behavioral finance also underscores the importance of data in modern investing. Understanding the psychological factors that influence investor behavior can help in crafting strategies that mitigate emotional decision-making. Data-driven insights into market sentiment can reveal patterns that suggest when investors are overly optimistic or pessimistic, providing opportunities to capitalize on market inefficiencies. By integrating behavioral data into their analyses, investors can make more rational choices, ultimately enhancing their long-term performance and mitigating risks associated with market volatility.

Moreover, the advent of technology has revolutionized how investors access and analyze data. Real-time market analysis tools allow for immediate reactions to market changes, making it essential for day traders and stock brokers to stay informed and agile. Leveraging technology to gather and interpret data not only improves decision-making speed but also enriches the depth of analysis available to investors. As data continues to grow in importance, those who can effectively utilize technology to harness this information will have a significant advantage in identifying emerging markets and trends across asset classes.

Lastly, the ethical considerations surrounding data use in real estate and tech investments cannot be overlooked. Investors must navigate the fine line between leveraging data for competitive advantage and ensuring that their practices align with ethical standards. Sustainable investing strategies, for instance, rely on accurate data to assess the impact of investments on society and the environment. By prioritizing transparency and ethical practices, investors can not only enhance their reputations but also contribute positively to the communities they operate within. As such, integrating data analytics while adhering to ethical principles is vital for long-term success in the ever-evolving investment landscape.

Tools and Techniques for Data-Driven Investment

In the realm of data-driven investment, leveraging the right tools and techniques is essential for success across various asset classes, including real estate, stocks, and technology. Investors today have access to an unprecedented amount of data, and utilizing advanced analytics tools can significantly enhance decision-making processes. These tools range from comprehensive financial analysis software to specialized market research platforms, each designed to provide insights that can guide investment strategies. By integrating these tools into their workflows, investors can identify trends, evaluate risks, and make informed choices that align with their financial goals.

One effective technique for data-driven investing is the use of predictive analytics, which employs statistical algorithms and machine learning to forecast market trends. This approach allows investors to analyze historical data and model potential future outcomes. For instance, a real estate investor might use predictive analytics to assess which neighborhoods are likely to experience growth based on factors like historical appreciation rates, demographic shifts, and economic developments. Similarly, stock investors can apply these techniques to identify stocks with high growth potential by evaluating past performance metrics and current market conditions.

Another vital aspect of data-driven investment is the application of real-time market analysis tools. Investors can utilize platforms that aggregate market data, news, and social media sentiment to stay informed about market movements and emerging trends. These tools provide a competitive edge, enabling investors to react quickly to changes in the market, whether they are aiming for short-term gains or long-term positions. For instance, day traders often rely on real-time data feeds to execute trades based on immediate market fluctuations, while long-term investors might monitor broader economic indicators to make strategic decisions.

Diversification is a fundamental principle of risk management, and data-driven techniques can help investors effectively diversify their portfolios across different asset classes. By analyzing correlations between various investments, investors can identify opportunities to reduce risk without sacrificing potential returns. Tools that facilitate asset allocation analysis enable investors to simulate different portfolio scenarios, allowing them to make adjustments based on changing market conditions or personal risk tolerance. This strategic approach to diversification can enhance overall portfolio performance, particularly in volatile markets.

Lastly, ethical considerations in investment practices are increasingly becoming a focal point for investors. Data-driven tools can also play a role in promoting sustainable and responsible investing. By utilizing platforms that provide environmental, social, and governance (ESG) metrics, investors can evaluate the ethical implications of their investment choices. This not only aligns with growing consumer demand for corporate responsibility but also helps investors identify companies that are likely to perform well in the long run due to their sustainable practices. Integrating such tools into investment strategies ensures that investors not only seek financial gains but also contribute positively to society and the environment.

Chapter 11: Strategies for Identifying Emerging Markets in Tech

Recognizing Trends and Opportunities

Recognizing trends and opportunities is crucial for success in the dynamic landscapes of real estate, stock, and tech investment. Investors must stay vigilant in monitoring economic indicators, market behaviors, and emerging technologies that can signal shifts in opportunities. By understanding the rhythm of the market, investors can position themselves to capitalize on lucrative investments before the broader market catches on. This involves not only analyzing current data but also interpreting historical trends to predict future movements.

A keen eye for detail and a proactive approach can help investors identify those critical moments that lead to strategic advantages.

Behavioral finance plays a significant role in recognizing trends. The psychology behind investor behavior can influence market movements, often leading to irrational decisions that create opportunities for savvy investors. By understanding common psychological traps—such as herd mentality or overreaction to news—investors can position themselves to take advantage of market anomalies. This insight allows for tactical decision-making that leverages investor sentiment, presenting opportunities that may not be immediately evident through traditional analysis.

Incorporating technology into investment strategies enhances the ability to recognize trends and opportunities in real-time. Advanced analytics, machine learning, and big data tools allow investors to process vast amounts of information quickly. This technological edge offers insights into market movements, consumer behavior, and investment performance, enabling investors to make informed decisions based on up-to-date data. Such tools not only improve the accuracy of predictions but also assist in identifying emerging markets within the tech industry, where rapid innovation can lead to significant returns.

Sustainable investing has also become a focal point for many investors, particularly in the tech and real estate sectors. Recognizing the growing demand for environmentally responsible and socially conscious investments can reveal new opportunities. Companies that prioritize sustainability often attract more investors and customers, leading to enhanced financial performance. Real estate investors can leverage this trend by focusing on properties that promote energy efficiency or community well-being, thereby appealing to a market that increasingly values ethical considerations.

Diversification across asset classes remains a fundamental strategy for managing risk while recognizing trends and opportunities. By spreading investments across real estate, stocks, and tech, investors can mitigate potential losses from market volatility. Furthermore, understanding the correlation between different asset classes allows for more effective allocation of resources, ensuring that investors can capitalize on the strengths of each sector while protecting their portfolios from downturns. This approach enables investors to remain agile and responsive to market changes, maximizing the potential for long-term success.

Assessing Market Viability and Growth Potential

Assessing market viability and growth potential is crucial for investors seeking to maximize their returns across various asset classes, including real estate, stocks, and technology. This process begins with a comprehensive analysis of market trends, economic indicators, and consumer behavior. Real estate investors must consider factors such as rental demand, property values, and demographic shifts, while stock and tech investors should pay close attention to industry innovations, market cycles, and competitive landscapes. By understanding these elements, investors can identify opportunities that align with their goals and risk appetites.

One of the essential tools in assessing market viability is the evaluation of economic indicators. These indicators, such as GDP growth rates, unemployment levels, and inflation, provide insights into the overall health of the economy. For example, a rising GDP typically signals a robust economy, which can lead to increased consumer spending and higher demand for both real estate and tech products. Conversely, high unemployment rates may suggest economic instability, impacting investor confidence and market performance. By analyzing these indicators, investors can make informed decisions about when to enter or exit specific markets.

In addition to economic indicators, behavioral finance plays a significant role in understanding market dynamics. Investors must recognize the psychological factors that can influence market trends and investor decisions. For instance, market sentiment often drives stock prices, with fear and greed leading to irrational behaviors. By being aware of these psychological triggers, investors can better navigate market fluctuations and identify potentially undervalued assets. This awareness is particularly important in the tech sector, where innovation cycles can create volatility that savvy investors can exploit.

Technology has revolutionized the way investors assess market viability. Advanced data analytics tools and real-time market analysis platforms allow investors to gather and interpret vast amounts of data quickly. These technologies enable the identification of emerging markets and trends that may not be apparent through traditional analysis methods. By leveraging these tools, investors can enhance their decision-making processes and develop strategies that capitalize on market shifts before their competitors. This proactive approach is essential for achieving sustainable growth and maximizing investment returns.

Lastly, diversification remains a key strategy in mitigating risk and enhancing growth potential. By spreading investments across various asset classes, including stocks, tech, and real estate, investors can reduce exposure to any single market's volatility. This technique not only protects against downturns but also positions investors to benefit from the different growth trajectories of each asset class. Moreover, ethical considerations in real estate investment practices and sustainable investing strategies in tech further underscore the importance of a holistic approach to market assessment. By prioritizing these strategies, investors can align their portfolios with both their financial goals and their values, ultimately fostering long-term success in the ever-evolving investment landscape.

Chapter 12: Ethical Considerations in Real Estate Investment Practices

Understanding Ethical Investing in Real Estate

Understanding ethical investing in real estate involves recognizing the intersection of financial returns and social responsibility. Ethical investing prioritizes investments that positively impact society and the environment, going beyond merely seeking profit. This approach applies to real estate by considering how properties can contribute to community well-being, environmental sustainability, and equitable economic development. Investors must assess not only the financial metrics of a property but also its broader implications for the community and the planet.

One key aspect of ethical investing in real estate is the focus on sustainable development practices. This includes investing in properties that utilize green building materials, energy-efficient technologies, and sustainable land-use practices. By promoting environmentally friendly developments, investors can reduce their carbon footprint while appealing to a growing market of eco-conscious tenants and buyers. Furthermore, properties that incorporate sustainable practices often experience lower operational costs and higher long-term value, aligning ethical principles with sound investment strategies.

Another critical consideration is social equity within the communities where real estate investments are made. Ethical investors evaluate how their projects affect local populations, particularly marginalized groups. This means supporting affordable housing initiatives, fostering inclusive community development, and engaging with local residents in the planning process. By prioritizing social equity, investors can help address housing shortages and promote economic stability, ultimately leading to more resilient communities and potentially enhancing property values.

Investors must also be aware of the regulatory landscape surrounding ethical investing in real estate. Government policies increasingly favor sustainable and socially responsible practices, offering incentives such as tax breaks or grants for projects that meet certain criteria. Understanding these regulations allows investors to align their strategies with current trends and benefit from government support, while also contributing to positive societal outcomes. Knowledge of local zoning laws, environmental regulations, and community development policies is essential for ethical real estate investing.

Finally, ethical investing in real estate requires a commitment to ongoing education and awareness of emerging trends. Investors should stay informed about the latest developments in sustainability, social justice, and community engagement. By leveraging technology and data analytics, investors can assess potential investments' social and environmental impacts effectively. This proactive approach not only enhances investment decisions but also ensures that investors can adapt to evolving market demands and societal expectations, ultimately fostering a more sustainable and equitable real estate sector.

Navigating Legal and Moral Implications in Real Estate Investments

Navigating the legal and moral implications of real estate investments is a critical aspect for investors aiming to achieve long-term success. As the real estate market continues to evolve, understanding the regulatory framework is essential. Investors must familiarize themselves with local, state, and federal laws that govern property transactions, zoning regulations, and landlord-tenant relationships. Compliance with these regulations not only mitigates legal risks but also enhances the investor's credibility in the market. Additionally, staying informed about changes in legislation, such as property tax laws or environmental regulations, can provide a competitive edge and prevent costly legal disputes.

Beyond legalities, ethical considerations play a significant role in real estate investing. Investors must reflect on the impact of their decisions on the communities in which they operate. Ethical investing practices involve being transparent in dealings, treating tenants and buyers fairly, and considering the social implications of property development. For instance, gentrification can lead to displacement of long-time residents, raising moral questions about the investor's role in community transformation. By prioritizing ethical practices, investors can foster positive relationships with stakeholders and contribute to sustainable community development, ultimately enhancing their reputation and business longevity.

Another crucial aspect is the consideration of sustainable investing strategies in real estate. Investors are increasingly recognizing the importance of environmental, social, and governance (ESG) criteria in their investment decisions. Properties that incorporate energy-efficient technologies or sustainable materials not only appeal to environmentally conscious buyers but also often benefit from reduced operating costs in the long run. By aligning investment strategies with sustainability goals, investors can contribute to a healthier planet while potentially increasing the value of their portfolios. This approach not only addresses moral imperatives but also responds to a growing demand in the market for eco-friendly properties.

Furthermore, behavioral finance can provide insights into the psychological factors that influence investment decisions. Understanding cognitive biases can help investors navigate the complexities of the real estate market. For instance, overconfidence may lead an investor to overlook critical due diligence, while loss aversion might prevent them from making necessary adjustments to their portfolio. By recognizing these biases and employing strategies to counteract them, investors can enhance their decision-making processes and reduce the likelihood of costly mistakes. This knowledge is particularly valuable in volatile markets where emotions can cloud judgment.

Finally, leveraging technology for real-time market analysis can significantly aid investors in navigating the legal and moral implications of their investments. Advanced data analytics tools can provide insights into market trends, property values, and demographic shifts, allowing investors to make informed decisions. By utilizing technology to monitor compliance with legal requirements and assess the potential social impact of their investments, investors can better align their strategies with both legal standards and ethical norms. This integration of technology not only streamlines the investment process but also positions investors to make choices that are both profitable and socially responsible.

Chapter 13: Conclusion: The Path to Investment Mastery

Recap of Key Strategies

In the realm of investing, mastering key strategies is crucial for navigating the complexities of stock, tech, and real estate markets. One of the foundational strategies is diversification across asset classes. By spreading investments across various sectors—such as stocks, real estate, and technology—investors can mitigate risks associated with market volatility. Diversification not only enhances the potential for returns but also provides a buffer against unexpected downturns in any single market. Understanding the correlation between different asset classes enables investors to build a balanced portfolio that responds resiliently to market fluctuations.

Sustainable investing strategies have gained prominence, particularly in the tech and real estate sectors. Investors are increasingly focusing on companies and projects that prioritize environmental, social, and governance (ESG) criteria. This approach not only aligns with ethical considerations but also taps into a growing consumer preference for sustainable practices. Identifying investments that adhere to these principles can yield long-term benefits, as businesses that prioritize sustainability often demonstrate better risk management and adaptability in changing market conditions. As a result, integrating sustainability into investment strategies can enhance both profitability and societal impact.

Behavioral finance plays a significant role in understanding how psychology influences investment decisions. Successful investors often exhibit traits such as discipline, patience, and the ability to manage emotions in the face of market fluctuations. Recognizing common cognitive biases—such as overconfidence or loss aversion—can empower investors to make more rational decisions. Developing a strong psychological framework can lead to better investment outcomes, as it encourages a focus on long-term goals rather than short-term market noise. Training oneself to approach investing with a clear and objective mindset can significantly improve overall performance.

The impact of economic indicators on stock market decisions cannot be overstated. Factors such as interest rates, inflation, and unemployment rates provide essential insights into market trends and potential investment opportunities. Savvy investors stay informed about these indicators and utilize them to guide their decision-making processes. For instance, a rising interest rate may signal a shift in market sentiment, prompting investors to reevaluate their positions. Understanding these economic signals, combined with real-time market analysis tools, allows investors to make informed choices that align with prevailing market conditions.

Finally, leveraging technology for real-time market analysis has become indispensable for modern investors. Advanced data analytics tools enable investors to track market trends, analyze performance metrics, and identify emerging markets in technology. By utilizing algorithms and machine learning, investors can gain insights that were previously unavailable, allowing for more informed investment strategies. Furthermore, the ability to perform rapid analysis fosters a proactive approach to investment management, ensuring that investors can quickly adapt to changing market dynamics and seize new opportunities as they arise. Adopting these technological advancements can greatly enhance an investor's strategy and overall success in the market.

Developing a Continuous Learning Mindset

Developing a continuous learning mindset is essential for success in the dynamic landscape of real estate and stock investing. The market is ever-evolving, influenced by economic indicators, technological advancements, and shifts in consumer behavior. Investors who adopt a mindset focused on lifelong learning are better equipped to adapt to these changes and to make informed decisions. This mindset encourages the pursuit of knowledge from various sources, enabling investors to stay ahead of trends and recognize potential opportunities in both established and emerging markets.

One of the key components of a continuous learning mindset is the ability to analyze and interpret data effectively. In today's investing environment, leveraging technology for real-time market analysis is crucial. Investors must familiarize themselves with data analytics tools that provide insights into market trends, asset performance, and economic factors. By understanding how to extract actionable information from data, investors can enhance their decision-making processes. This analytical approach not only aids in identifying promising investment opportunities but also helps in assessing risks associated with different asset classes.

Behavioral finance plays a significant role in shaping investment strategies. Understanding the psychology of successful investors involves recognizing biases and emotional triggers that can impact decision-making. Continuous learning fosters self-awareness and critical thinking, allowing investors to reflect on their own behaviors and the behaviors of the market. By studying past market cycles and investor reactions, one can develop a more nuanced perspective on risk management and investment timing, leading to more strategic long-term and short-term investment decisions.

Moreover, investors must remain informed about sustainable investing strategies, especially in the realms of tech and real estate. As societal values shift towards sustainability, understanding the implications of these changes on investment practices is paramount. Continuous learning enables investors to explore ethical considerations in their investment choices, ensuring that their portfolios not only yield financial returns but also contribute positively to society. By keeping abreast of new regulations, green technologies, and sustainable practices, investors can position themselves as leaders in responsible investing.

Finally, cultivating a continuous learning mindset encourages diversification across asset classes. With the market's inherent volatility, relying solely on one type of investment can be risky. Investors should actively seek knowledge about various sectors, including real estate and technology, to identify diversification techniques that mitigate risk while maximizing potential gains. By fostering relationships within the investment community and participating in educational opportunities, such as workshops and seminars, investors can expand their knowledge base and enhance their ability to navigate the complexities of the market effectively.

www.ingramcontent.com/pod-product-compliance
Lightning Source LLC
Chambersburg PA
CBHW070950220526
45471CB00007B/2963